IMAGES
of America

NEWTON

"Newton has won an enviable reputation as a desirable place of residence . . ."—Mayor J. Wesley Kimball, Inaugural Address, 1887.

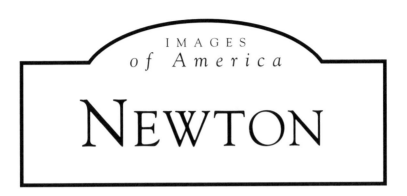

IMAGES
of America

NEWTON

Thelma Fleishman
for the Newton Historical Society

ARCADIA

Published by Arcadia Publishing,
an imprint of Tempus Publishing, Inc.
2 Cumberland Street
Charleston, SC 29401

Printed in Great Britain.

Library of Congress Catalog Card Number: Applied for.

For all general information contact Arcadia Publishing at:
Telephone 843-853-2070
Fax 843-853-0044
E-Mail arcadia@charleston.net

For customer service and orders:
Toll-Free 1-888-313-BOOK

Visit us on the internet at http://www.arcadiaimages.com

CONTENTS

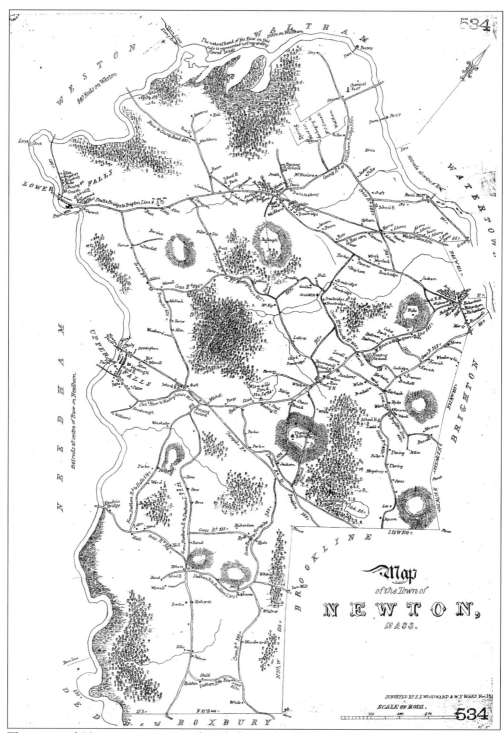

This map of Newton was surveyed and drawn by local residents Elijah Woodward and William Ward in 1831, when the possibility of a railroad from Boston to the west was under consideration.

One

BEFORE THE RAILROAD

When Elijah Woodward and William Ward prepared their map of Newton in 1831, there was no obvious town center. About a third of the homesteads were scattered along the town and county ways; the rest were clustered in five villages: Newton Corner, Newton Centre, West Newton, Newton Upper Falls, and Newton Lower Falls. Newton Corner, then called Angier's Corner after the local innkeeper, was the oldest.

Settlement had begun near the Brighton line in the 1630s, when this area south of the Charles River was still part of Cambridge. A generation later, because of the distance they had to travel to the meetinghouse near the Cambridge Common for town meetings and religious services, several families sought permission to conduct the latter separately. Eventually, permission was granted, and, in 1660, they built a meetinghouse and established a burying place at the corner of Centre and Cotton Streets. In 1688, what had become known as Cambridge Village was incorporated as the Town of Newton. Within a few years, the school, the training field, and the pound were all located nearby, completing what was, briefly, the town "center."

In 1711, some families that had settled farther afield complained of the difficulties of winter travel to the meetinghouse and petitioned the Massachusetts General Court for permission to have it moved to a more convenient site. After several years of bitter exchanges between residents living in the northern and southern parts of town, a surveyor was appointed to determine its geographical center. The new meetinghouse that was built in 1721 at the corner of Centre and Homer Streets, became the nucleus of a new village. Newton Centre would be the town center for more than a century.

By the mid-1700s, there were the beginnings of a village where the highways from surrounding towns converged at what would become West Newton Square. In 1764, because the terrain made travel to the meetinghouse in the Centre difficult, local residents built their own house of worship, and, in 1781, the Second (or West) Parish was incorporated. This was a major step in the development of the village of West Newton, which, in due course, would succeed Newton Centre as the town's administrative center and serve as such for nearly a century.

Meanwhile, there had been mills on the Charles River at Newton Upper and Lower Falls since the late 17th and early 18th centuries respectively. Operated as family concerns for decades, mill production increased at both sites during the Industrial Revolution so that two thriving, largely self-contained villages had developed by the 1830s.

Industrial activity was not confined to the Falls. After the end of the American Revolution, several mostly smaller mills and factories were established in different parts of town, manufacturing and sometimes exporting products as varied as candles, glue, furniture, chemicals, and dyestuffs. What is sometimes referred to as Newton's Industrial Period lasted for half a century, until the 1830s, when the introduction of rail service to Boston ushered in a new era.

The East Parish Burying Ground at Centre and Cotton Streets is the resting-place of many of the founding families whose names are familiar as Newton's streets, schools, and ponds. In 1852, descendants of the first settlers erected the obelisk in the background to mark the site of the first meetinghouse.

Thomas Greenwood, who died in 1774, was town clerk and treasurer for 23 years. His grave marker is the work of well-known carver Daniel Hastings who lived and worked in Newton Corner. (Photograph courtesy of Steve Rosenthal.)

Judge Abraham Fuller followed Greenwood as town clerk and treasurer. Besides being a judge, he represented Newton in the Massachusetts General Court and at the Provincial Congress. When he died, he left 300 pounds "for the foundation of an Academy in Newton."

Sarah and Abraham Fuller lived on the farm in Newtonville that had belonged to Abraham's father and grandfather. One of the town's largest, it extended from Newtonville Square to Beacon Street. Both portraits were painted by John Johnston in 1790.

William Hull opened a law practice in Newton Corner after a distinguished military career in the American Revolution. In 1805, he was sent to the Michigan Territory as its first governor. Reluctantly assuming command of the troops when war broke out in 1812, he was court-martialed for surrendering Detroit to the British. Pardoned by President Madison, he returned to Newton in 1814. Both portraits were painted by James Sharples.

One of the two Newton chapters of the Daughters of the American Revolution was named after Sarah Hull. The daughter of Sarah and Abraham Fuller, she married William Hull in 1781. She accompanied him wherever his military duties took him until they settled in Newton after the American Revolution. They lived in the original brick section of Nonantum House in Newton Corner until her father died and she inherited the Fuller farm in Newtonville.

The Nonantum House served many purposes after the Hulls left. Enlarged in 1837, it remained a landmark in Newton Corner until the 1930s.

In her time, Susanna Rowson was well known as a novelist. For some years in the early 1800s, she ran a school in the Nonantum House. It was one of the country's earliest boarding establishments for young ladies. (Courtesy Boston Athenaeum.)

The "Old Meeting House" in Newton Centre was sketched from memory by Nancy Freeman Clarke (the Hulls' granddaughter) in 1889. It was the second of four buildings on the site (at the corner of Centre and Homer Streets) that had been determined to be the geographical center of the town in 1721.

The Newton Theological Institution was the first Baptist seminary in the country. In 1829, the institution bought 85 acres in Newton Centre on what would become Institution Hill. Shown in this 1839 woodcut is Farwell Hall, built that same year, and the mansion house of the property's former owner, John Peck.

Marshall Rice settled in Newton Centre in 1826 and was soon deeply involved in the affairs of both the village and the town. He ran a boarding school for boys, was an incorporator of the Newton Centre Tree Club, and, as a surveyor, was responsible for a large number of Newton's 19th-century land plans.

Although the town house was moved from Newton Centre to West Newton in 1848, Marshall Rice ran his office as town clerk and treasurer from his home on Centre Street until Newton became a city. The house, photographed in the 1880s, was built by Henry Gibbs in 1742; it has since been demolished.

The first meetinghouse in the Second (or West) Parish was built in 1764 at the corner of Washington and Cherry Streets. The steeple was added when the building was enlarged in 1812; this pencil sketch by George Fuller shows the church edifice before further changes were made in 1831.

Until the 1860s, the building at 428 Cherry Street in West Newton was on Washington Street, approximately where the courthouse is now. It was built c. 1715 by William Williams, a cousin of the founder of Williams College.

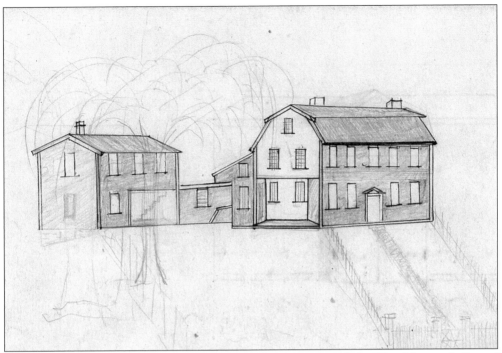

Seen above is "[t]he residence of Joseph Jackson Esq. Town Clerk, West Newton." One of several pencil sketches of the north side of Washington Street "as it appeared in 1828," was drawn later in the century by George Fuller. A harness-maker, Fuller had a shop on the opposite side of the street.

Seth Davis is said to have been penniless when he came to West Newton in 1802, but barely 20 years later, he was able to build this house at 32 Eden Road and, not long after, the Railway Hotel in West Newton Square.

The manufacture of textiles at Newton Upper Falls began in 1832, when Simon Elliot, financed by his father-in-law, Thomas Handasyd Perkins, erected the first brick cotton-mill in Newton. A second mill, shown above, was built in 1825. It has been converted to commercial use. Perkins endowed the Perkins School for the Blind in Watertown.

The Second Baptist Church in Newton was built in Newton Upper Falls in 1833.

Otis Pettee came to Upper Falls to supervise operations at the Elliot Mills. After a few years, he left to start his own plant for making textile manufacturing machinery on South Meadow Brook. This business was so successful that, in 1840, he was able to buy the Elliot Mills. By the time he died in 1853, his mills were among the largest textile-manufacturing concerns in New England. He built "Sunnyside" on Elliot Street in 1828. Bought as a home for "aged people" by the Stone Institute in 1895, the building is part of a life care complex.

This modest stone building on Washington Street was built *c.* 1830. It is all that remains of the mills in Newton Lower Falls, which were once so numerous that the amount of water power that each could use had to be regulated.

Wales's Tavern stood on the triangle formed by the Charles River, Washington, and Wales Streets in Newton Lower Falls. Opened in 1750 by Ephraim Jackson, it was owned and run by Nathaniel Wales from 1803 until his death in 1864, the year William Hollis drew this image. The building was destroyed by fire in 1867.

The Reverend Alfred Baury was the rector of St. Mary's Episcopal Church in Newton Lower Falls from 1822 to 1851. His rectory, much altered at 1245 Washington Street, was the headquarters of the Lucy Jackson Chapter of the Daughters of the American Revolution for many years.

St. Mary's was the first Episcopal congregation west of Boston. Erected in 1813, the church is the oldest religious building in Newton.

Seth Bemis owned mill complexes on both sides of the Charles River in the North Village (now Nonantum), where his father had started manufacturing paper in the 1770s.

Bemis rebuilt the dam and the paper mill on the Newton bank, *c.* 1820. The dam was damaged in the 1940s. It is now under the control of the Metropolitan District Commission, which has left the breach to provide a passage for migrating fish. (Photograph courtesy of Steve Rosenthal.)

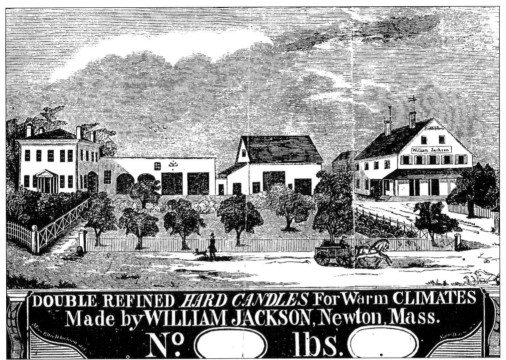

William Jackson opened a soap and candle factory on Washington Street in the 1820s. By the 1840s, he was exporting his products to Europe and the West Indies. The label, a stylized rendering of Jackson's house, barn, and factory was designed by his daughter Ellen.

The same view as the label, this is reproduced from a daguerreotype taken in the late 1840s. The house, built in 1809 by William's father, Timothy, currently accommodates Newton's Museum and Historical Society. The candle business was moved to Brighton in the 1870s.

THE

NEW AMERICAN ORCHARDIST,

OR

AN ACCOUNT OF THE MOST

VALUABLE VARIETIES OF FRUIT,

OF ALL CLIMATES,

ADAPTED TO CULTIVATION

IN

THE UNITED STATES,

WITH THEIR HISTORY, MODES OF CULTURE, MANAGEMENT,
USES, &c.

AND

THE CULTURE OF SILK.

WITH AN APPENDIX ON

VEGETABLES,

ORNAMENTAL TREES, SHRUBS AND FLOWERS.

BY WILLIAM KENRICK.

SECOND EDITION, ENLARGED AND IMPROVED.

———◆———

BOSTON:
RUSSELL, ODIORNE, AND METCALF,
AND GEORGE C. BARRETT.
1835.

William Kenrick, a founding member of the Massachusetts Horticultural Society, was well known for importing and propagating new strains of fruit trees. One of the first in New England, his nursery on Nonantum (now Farlow) Hill was started by his father in 1790.

Thomas Smallwood came from England in 1817, settled in Newton Corner, and started making furniture soon after his arrival. When his son Edwin took over the business in 1846, he built the new factory on Waverley Avenue, shown here before 1875.

In this portrait of the Smallwood family in the 1850s, Thomas sits in the center; Edwin stands to his right.

Of several first period houses still standing in Newton, the Hammond House at 9 Old Orchard Road in Chestnut Hill is the oldest. Built *c.* 1661 by Thomas Hammond Jr. (son of the Thomas who gave his name to Hammond Pond), the house was extensively altered in the 1930s.

The Murdock-Wiswall house was built *c.* 1720 by Robert Murdock; it was then owned by the Wiswall family from 1767 until 1858. Shown here in its original location on the corner of Dedham and Brookline Streets at the foot of Oak Hill, it has since been moved to Carlson Avenue on the grounds of Mt. Ida College. The house now serves as the official residence of the college president.

The first settlers in what became Waban were John and Rebecca Woodward, who built this house at 50 Fairlee Road in 1681. Their descendants, including Elijah, who surveyed the town in 1831, lived here until the 1950s.

William Robinson built his house at 473 Auburn Street in Auburndale, c. 1724. It is known both as the Whittemore Tavern because of the inn kept there in the 1760s, and as the Bourne House after the brothers who bought it in 1843.

In the late 1820s, besides managing his candle factory, William Jackson actively promoted the construction of a railroad, rather than a canal, to connect Boston with the west. He was largely instrumental in having the tracks routed through Newton and, subsequently, was the developer of the town's first residential subdivision.

Two
TRAINS AND TROLLEYS

In May 1834, the Boston and Worcester Railroad began running three trains a day between Boston and Newton. Ten years later, the introduction of faster and more frequent service led to the auction of lots in Newton's first suburban subdivision. "Walnut Park" was soon followed by others in Newton Corner, West Newton, and in Newtonville and Auburndale, the two new villages that developed along the tracks.

Initially, no provision had been made for moving freight from the mills at either Newton Upper or Lower Falls. To remedy this omission, a spur was built between the main line near Riverside and Newton Lower Falls in 1840. In 1852, the Charles River Railroad, which had previously terminated in Brookline, was extended through Newton to Newton Upper Falls. Although there were stops at Chestnut Hill, Newton Centre, and Newton Highlands (part of the general area known as Oak Hill), there was little development along this line until after 1870, when gravel trains carrying fill from Needham to Boston's Back Bay ceased operation.

In 1869, the Boston and Worcester Railroad absorbed the Western Railroad to become the Boston and Albany. In 1882, the company laid an additional set of tracks paralleling the main line to carry suburban traffic through Newton, and having bought the old Charles River Railroad, built an extension from Newton Highlands to join the new suburban tracks at Riverside. This completed a circuit. At the same time, several new stations were built; some followed the plans of Henry Hobson Richardson with landscaping by Frederick Law Olmsted. With additional stops at Woodland, Eliot, and Waban on the southern or Highland Branch, the Circuit Railroad went into operation in 1886, triggering a period of accelerated growth in Newton that lasted, almost unchecked, until World War I.

By the 1890s, the railroad crossings, particularly in the village centers, were becoming increasingly dangerous; the need to separate locomotives from other forms of transportation and pedestrians became urgent. After careful study, it was decided that lowering the tracks would decrease the risk. Work on the main line began in 1895; work on the Highland Branch began ten years later.

Street railways had little impact on residential development in Newton. Although some lines provided an alternate (and cheaper) means of transport to Boston, most served primarily to connect the villages with each other and outlying areas with the railroad stations.

A horse-drawn street car line between Boston and Watertown passed through Newton Corner as early as 1857; the first local line, between West Newton and Waltham, opened in 1866 and was followed soon after by service from Newton Corner to Newtonville and West Newton. At the century's end, there were seven lines operating in Newton (all electrified by the 1890s), which belonged to an ever-changing number of companies. These were all eventually absorbed by the Boston and Middlesex Street Railway Company.

Seth Davis's Railroad Hotel in West Newton can be seen in this 1890s photograph. Here, on April 7, 1834, the directors of the Boston and Worcester Railroad and 50 guests, the first passengers to have made the journey by train, celebrated their safe arrival in West Newton at this hotel.

By May 1834, the *Meteor* and its companion the *Rocket* were providing three round trips a day between Boston and West Newton. The fare was 37.5¢ each way.

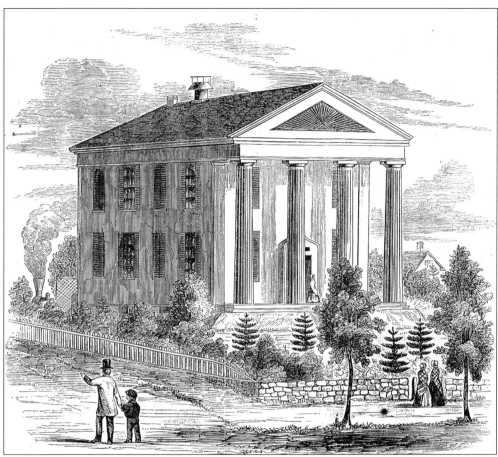

Educational institutions were quick to recognize the advantages of the "special," more frequent passenger service to Newton that was introduced in 1843. Horace Mann moved the State Normal School for Girls into the vacant Fuller Academy, which, as the engraving published in *Gleason's* *Pictorial Drawing Room Companion* shows, abutted the tracks in West Newton. Initially constructed with funds bequeathed by Judge Fuller, the building was taken over by Nathaniel T. Allen's West Newton English and Classical School in 1853.

m. a sketch by A. Conant.

The novelty of the railroad and the satisfaction at having it routed through Newton persisted for several years. The advantages of commuter service to Boston was brought to the notice of the public whenever possible, and developers used its availability to "puff up" sales. (Only

WTON CORNER.

ISKE HILL.

Nathaniel Hawthorne, who lived briefly on West Newton Hill in the 1850s, complained of the noise and the soot.) In this 1851 "[v]iew of Newton Corner [f]rom Fiske Hill" (now Mount Ida), the train is shown shortly after leaving the station.

The Boston and Worcester Railroad chose "Newton Corner" as the name of the station at what was then known as "Angier's Corner." In 1870, the newly chartered Boston and Albany changed it to simply "Newton." This photograph was taken before the second pair of tracks to Riverside was laid in 1882.

In 1842, a flag stop was introduced about halfway between Newton Corner and West Newton. Known at the time as Hull's Crossing, it later became Newtonville. The village square is shown here in the 1870s.

Another flag stop, between West Newton and Riverside, served the embryonic village of Auburndale. Here, "on the line of the Worcester Railroad ten miles from Boston," Edward Lasell started his Female Seminary in 1851. Bragdon Hall, the institution's first building, is shown (much enlarged) as it looked in the 1880s.

The depot, shown here in the 1890s, was built shortly after 1852 when Otis Pettee persuaded the Charles River Railroad to extend its tracks from Brookline through Newton to his mills in Newton Upper Falls.

The engraving, showing the train traveling to Boston on the newly extended Charles River Railroad, embellished a plan issued in 1856 to promote lot sales in "Chestnut Hill." The developers of what was at the time the largest subdivision in Newton were the heirs of Joseph Lee, the last owner of the original Hammond Farm.

This is Newtonville Station, post-1882, when the Boston and Albany Railroad had laid an additional set of tracks to carry suburban traffic through Newton to Riverside.

The Circuit Railroad was completed in 1886. The extension of the Charles River Railroad, known as the Highland Branch (now used by the D cars on the Green Line), can be seen in the foreground. The tracks of the main line to the west cross the photograph diagonally, and in the upper left-hand corner, the single-track spur to the Lower Falls depot in Wellesley makes a sharp curve to the right.

The names for two of the new stations on the Highland Branch, Waban and Eliot, were chosen by William C. Strong. Before moving to Newton, Strong lived in Brighton on Nonantum Hill, where the Reverend John Eliot, known as "the Apostle to the Indians," had preached to Waban and his band. Designed by local architect Lewis Bacon in 1896, Strong's Block, shown here *c.* 1920, was the first building in Waban Square.

This 1891 view of Newton Highlands was taken from the vicinity of Eliot Station. The spire of the Newton Highlands Congregational Church is just visible in the background on the extreme right.

The station at Chestnut Hill, designed by H.H. Richardson with landscaping by Frederick Law Olmsted, was one of several that attracted "the attention of the entire country to the Railroad Gardening of the Boston & Albany."—*Suburban Life*.

Before he died in 1886, Richardson completed plans for five Newton stations. Of these, only Woodland survives. The property of the Woodland Golf Club, it is used as a storage facility.

The potential for conflict between pedestrians, trains, and other vehicular traffic was causing alarm when this picture of Newton Corner was taken in the early 1890s.

On the Highland Branch, the need for the elimination of grade crossings was less urgent, as evidenced by this photograph taken at Cook Street in Newton Highlands.

In 1895, work began on lowering the tracks between Newton Corner and Riverside. (Boston and Albany Railroad Collection, courtesy Society for the Preservation of New England Antiquities [SPNEA].)

The Highland Branch was not depressed until ten years later. In this 1907 photograph, Newton Centre station can be seen from the west, while the steps down to the new platform were being built. (Boston and Albany Railroad Collection, courtesy SPNEA.)

Work can be seen in progress on the shores of Crystal Lake. (Boston and Albany Railroad Collection, courtesy SPNEA.)

Pictured here are the West Newton station and the newly built Chestnut Street bridge over the tracks.

This photograph of the Newton Centre station was taken several decades after the tracks were lowered. (Courtesy the Clark family.)

From the 1890s, it was possible to travel between Newton and Boston by electric trolley, which was less expensive, but slower, than the train. The Commonwealth Avenue Street Railway extended its service from Lake Street on the Boston line, shown here, down the new "boulevard" as far as Newton Centre in 1896.

Later that year, the line reached the Charles River in Auburndale; the following spring, the street car company opened Norumbega Park.

The Worcester Turnpike, laid out in 1808, was one of the first toll roads in New England. In 1901, it was reconstructed to carry the fast Inter-Urban "Air Line" Trolley, shown in Newton Upper Falls on its way to Boston. The Metropolitan Circular Dam, to the right of the bridge between Wellesley and Newton, was rebuilt in 1906.

The Air Line ran between Boston and Worcester for 30 years. In 1932, the tracks were taken up, and the roadway was reconstructed once more to become Route 9.

The Newton and Boston Street Railway ran cars from Boston along North Beacon Street to Watertown Street in Nonantum, shown here *c.* 1915, and then on to Newtonville Square. (Courtesy SPNEA.)

From Newtonville Square, there were trolleys to almost anywhere in the city; this one is on its way to Newton Corner. In 1905, the local post office, the streetcar waiting room, and a public telephone station were located in the Central Block (the building on the corner).

A trolley on Washington Street, en route from Newtonville to West Newton, passes the Newton Street Railway car barn.

Copyright 1905 by the Rotograph Co.

A 6967   Odd Fellows Hall, City Hall and 2nd Congregational Church, West Newton, Mass.

Will you exchange with one? Bro. Kellar, 182 Webster St.

None of the buildings seen in this 1905 photograph of West Newton Square still stand, including the Oddfellows Hall, the city hall, or the Second Church in Newton. After leaving the square, the trolley proceeded along Washington Street to Newton Lower Falls.

Some cars traveled south from Newtonville along Walnut Street. From the late 1890s until the 1920s, the passengers' needs were served by a waiting room at the intersection with

Commonwealth Avenue, on what is now the site of city hall.

From the waiting room, some cars went along Homer Street to Newton Centre Square, shown here in 1905.

Other trolleys continued down Walnut Street, past the Newton Cemetery (where there was a small shelter), to Newton Highlands (shown here), then on to Newton Upper Falls, and, after 1906, across the Charles River to Needham. (Courtesy the Clark Family.)

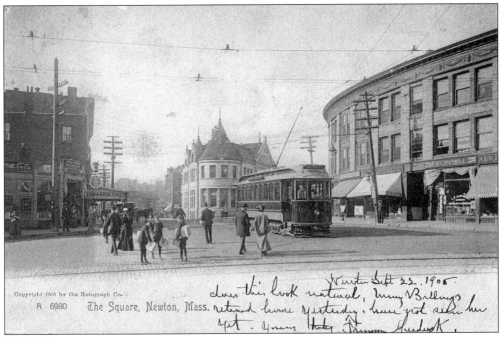

This postcard of Newton Corner dates from 1905. A daughter of Jewish immigrants living in Nonantum remembered that "every Saturday night you'd go to Newton Corner and take the street car to the West End [in Boston] and you'd buy all the things you needed for the week."

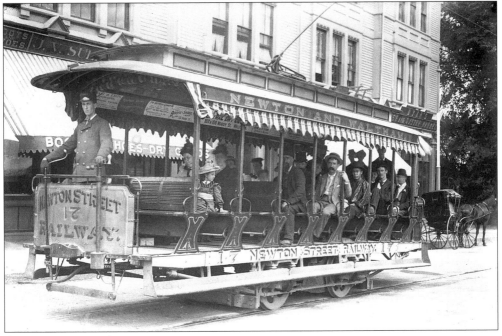

Open cars were used in summer.

By 1910, the Boston and Middlesex Street Railway Company had absorbed all the streetcar companies that had operated in Newton. Buses began replacing trolleys in the 1920s. (Courtesy the Clark family.)

Three
SUBURBAN LIVING

The practice of separating home from workplace, of retreating from the confines of the city to rural villages on the periphery, originated in late-18th-century England. It was adopted in this country by the 1820s and became more widespread in the following decade when the first railroads made "commuting" convenient.

Newton was among the first of America's railroad suburbs. Initially, the business and professional men who settled here were not native Bostonians "escaping" from the ills of their native city, but came from small New England towns. They bought lots in the new subdivisions; the houses that were built for them have left Newton with street after street of outstanding examples of 19th- and early-20th-century residential architecture. The newcomers soon outnumbered the long-established local families and became increasingly prominent in civic affairs as well as in the social, religious, philanthropic, and cultural organizations that proliferated in the 1880s and subsequent decades. Publications such as *An American Woman's Home* by Harriet Beecher Stowe and her sister Catherine in the 19th century and the monthly *Suburban Life* in the early 20th century influenced and reflected the attitudes of suburban dwellers towards almost everything, from the role of women as wives and mothers to the recreational possibilities of the automobile.

Years before Newton aspired to being "the Garden City of the Commonwealth," local developers and residents alike, in common with those in other rapidly expanding communities, recognized that the interests of all were best served by retaining or recreating surroundings reminiscent of the vanishing countryside. In advocating the "ornamentation of Roads, Lanes and Public Places" in the 1850s, the Newton Centre Tree Club revived an 18th-century practice of tree planting that would be continued by future improvement societies and eventually by the city. In a community that boasted one of the earliest commercial nurseries in New England, the interest in private gardens was fostered by the local Horticultural Society and village garden clubs.

Until well into the 20th century, Newton was perceived as a homogenous, upper-income, "WASP" community. But as substantial numbers of simple vernacular houses attest, not all who lived here were affluent, nor were they all Protestant, white, or Anglo-Saxon. The first Irish immigrants came in the 1840s, the oldest African-American community dates from the 1860s, and, by the 1890s, Nonantum, at least, had become home to French-Canadian, Italian, and Jewish families.

The automobile changed Newton for everyone. By introducing hitherto unfamiliar structures such as gas pumps and garages, by diminishing the need for local stores, and by making it feasible to live in outlying areas, the car opened a new phase of residential development.

By the 1860s, Newton Corner was the most populous village in Newton. This photograph, which shows the residential area on Centre Street south of the tracks, was taken before 1887, the year the Eliot Church was destroyed by fire.

This photograph of Newton Centre looks towards Boston along Beacon Street. It is one of several that Walter Claflin took in the 1890s from the tower of the Mason School. A parking lot currently occupies the site of the former school.

When this photograph of Pigeon Hill was taken in 1914, the large house in the center still belonged to the heirs of the Reverend Charles Dumaresque Pigeon. In 1847, Reverend Pigeon had persuaded the Boston and Worcester Railroad to introduce the local flag stop and was responsible for calling the resulting village "Auburn Dale."

In the 1890s, Newton Upper Falls, as seen here from the Needham end of Echo Bridge, was still a typical New England mill village; most of the residents worked in the mills.

Characteristic of early suburban development, these modest but elegant homes on Richardson Street, a block away from the Newton station, were built in the 1840s and '50s. Those on the right were demolished when the Massachusetts Turnpike was constructed.

Mature trees created an ideal suburban setting for single-family homes on Herrick Road in Newton Centre.

Nonantum, where successive waves of immigrants found their first homes, did not share all the amenities of the suburb. These houses are on Adams Street.

Some areas of Newton were untouched by suburban development. Beecher Place in Thompsonville was still semi-rural in the early decades of the 20th century.

Some 19th-century suburban homes have survived almost unchanged. Nathaniel T. Allen's house on Webster Street in West Newton is one of the few remaining high-style Greek Revival homes built in the 1840s. It was one of Newton's two documented stations on the Underground Railroad; the other was the Jackson Homestead.

The style known as Carpenter's Gothic is rare in Newton. The house at 106 Pleasant Street in Newton Centre was built by Charles S. Davis in the 1870s as a rental property.

J. Henry Bacon's house, at the corner of Bacon and Pearl Streets in Newton Corner, was one of many built with a mansard roof in the 1860s and early '70s. The photograph, taken in 1887, shows Bacon with his wife and her family.

Newton has an abundance of houses in the "Queen Anne" style, which was popular in the 1880s and '90s. This home of Boston businessman Frank J. Wetherell on Walnut Street in Newtonville was photographed on July 4, 1892. (Courtesy Joanne Baker.)

The elaborately landscaped garden of Charles and Mary Billings on Franklin Street in Newton Corner exemplified the "great care . . . lavished on the planting in private places." The photograph was taken in 1878.

Lawn tennis became increasingly popular in the 1890s. The players at "The Old Elms," the Newtonville estate of Governor William Claflin, are identified by initials only. Guests there sometimes included well-known personalities such as Harriet Beecher Stowe or Oliver Wendell Holmes. (Courtesy the Clark family.)

After the invention of the hand lawn mower in the mid-1800s made grass cutting easier, a trim lawn became the hallmark of a well-maintained suburban garden. Herbert Bacon, above, works at 40 Fairview Street in Newton Corner; below, Charles Read mows the lawn at 10 Chase Street in Newton Centre.

The Newell children are playing in the "pine grove" in the backyard of their home on Webster Street in West Newton.

This 1894 picture was taken on "[a] beautiful Sunday summer afternoon" at 1137 Boylston Street. "I well remember the flicker of light and shade and the very smell of the trodden grass . . ." narrates Edith Cobb Allen in 1959.

Julia Sweeney's yard, possibly the smallest in Newton, was wedged between Washington Street and the railroad. The house was removed when the street was widened and the tracks lowered in 1895.

Vestiges of the past lingered; Wauwinet Farm on Commonwealth Avenue in West Newton was one of the largest milk producers in the state until after World War I.

"For those whose inclinations or duties are home-bound, there is nothing that will yield quite so much delight . . . as a broad piazza or a porch." —*Suburban Life*. (Courtesy M. Russel Feldman.)

Adeline and Benjamin Franklin Bacon relax on their porch in Newton Corner in the early years of the 20th century.

The family of Adams Claflin posed on the steps of their home on Grant Avenue in Newton Centre.

Family and friends relax in the garden of the Jackson Homestead in the 1890s.

Private carriages were not uncommon; Mr. and Mrs. Charles Travelli can be seen with theirs in the 1890s. The carriage house survived the fire that destroyed the Travelli's home on Valentine Street in West Newton during a blizzard in 1888.

For those without their own means of transportation, there were hackney carriages, or "hacks," such as these awaiting fares outside the station in Newtonville in 1891.

In most villages, there were livery stables for transporting goods as well as people. This one, photographed in 1887, was run by Henry C. Daniels behind the Nonantum House in Newton Corner from 1837 until 1905.

Stores in the village commercial centers carried most items needed for everyday living. This image of the Hyde Block in Newton Corner was photographed in 1895.

This picture of a store in Newton Highlands was photographed in 1893.

The Barsam's Market in Auburndale was originally the railroad station; it was demolished to make way for the local branch library in 1928.

The depot for Hood's Dairy was on Bridge Street in Nonantum. The photograph was taken on Walnut Street in Newton Highlands in 1909.

Francis Edgar and Freelan Oscar Stanley are pictured in their first "Steamer," in 1897. The cars were made in Watertown, but both brothers lived in Newton Corner.

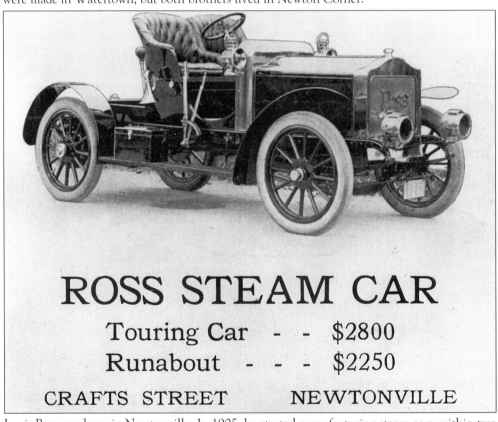

ROSS STEAM CAR
Touring Car - - $2800
Runabout - - - $2250
CRAFTS STREET   NEWTONVILLE

Louis Ross was born in Newtonville. In 1905, he started manufacturing steam cars; within two years, his factory was employing up to 40 hands. He was killed in 1927 while testing a radio torpedo signal.

Horses and the new horseless carriages shared the roads uneasily in this photograph of Newton Centre, in 1909.

The police department's first steamer and a street department team can be seen on Chestnut Street, in West Newton in 1902.

Soon automobiles were everywhere. Driving for pleasure became a popular pastime.

The Massachusetts Highway Association held a rally on Commonwealth Avenue in 1904.

As the automobile replaced the railroad as the dominant influence on development, hitherto unfamiliar structures appeared on city streets. A gas pump and automobile service station opened in a Newton Corner residential neighborhood in the early years of the 20th century.

New homes were designed to include shelters for automobiles.

For two decades, the Crowell Automobile Company occupied part of the city hall site on Commonwealth Avenue.

"The Newtons have done as much as any of the Boston suburbs in the way of beautifying their surroundings. But the work is constantly being spoilt by such encroachments."—*Suburban Life*, 1911. There were still billboards on Commonwealth Avenue when this photograph was taken in 1927.

"The problems which the automobile present are continually being studied . . ." stated Mayor Edwin Childs in 1926. Centre Street, approaching Washington Street in Newton Corner, was one of the trouble spots requiring "remedial steps." (The building on the right was Eliot Hall.)

These cars are parked in front of the high school on Walnut Street in the 1920s.

1915

AFTER THE SMASH · COM'TH AVE · NEAR CHESTNUT ST. Newton 245

The Newton Street Department took this photograph, titled *After the Smash*, in 1915.

By the second decade of the 20th century, special police officers were directing traffic. A new "traffic box" was installed in Newton Corner in 1931. (Courtesy the Clark family.)

A traffic beacon was located at the corner of Washington and Concord Streets in Lower Falls, 1929. The building on the left is Boyden Hall, designed by Alexander Esty in the 1850s. It was modernized in the 1940s.

The city authorized the first "fixed time traffic light" in December 1931, to be located at Commonwealth Avenue at Centre Street, a few months before this photograph was taken.

Four

PARKS AND PLAYGROUNDS

Shortly after its incorporation in 1829, the Massachusetts Horticultural Society voted to establish a cemetery combined with a botanical garden that would be more in keeping with the current attitudes towards death and nature than the old overcrowded Puritan burying grounds. Like Père Lachaise, then on the outskirts of Paris, it would be situated beyond the Boston city limits. The result was Mount Auburn in Cambridge, which over the years served as the model for other American garden cemeteries. The surveyor for Mount Auburn was Alexander Wadsworth, who, ten years later, drew the plans for at least six of Newton's earliest subdivisions, most with an oval park as a prominent feature.

Newton's garden cemetery on Walnut Street was incorporated in 1855. Like Mount Auburn, the landscaping owed much to the principles developed by the designers of 18th-century English country gardens; before long, its Picturesque-style carriage-ways and pedestrian paths became a popular weekend attraction. The number of visitors increased with the years, leading the president of the trustees to observe, in 1881, that "we, at the expense of our Proprietors make our grounds a *park* [his italics] for the City of Newton." The city appointed the first standing committee on parks the following year.

The committee submitted a report two years later. Expanding on a previous proposal for a series of parks between Chestnut Hill and West Newton, it recommended the acquisition of almost 400 acres extending from Valentine to Centre Streets, between Beacon Street and Bullough's Pond, for a single "Central Park." Although much of the survey work was completed, the scheme came to nothing. In 1885, however, plans were drawn for Newton's first public park on land given by John Farlow in Newton Corner; five years later the Newton Centre Improvement Association provided funds for the city's first public playground.

In the years that followed, the city acquired several parcels of parkland, some as large as Edmands Park, others little more than traffic islands. But by the turn of the 20th century, interest in passive recreation began to wane, and, as the playground movement gained momentum nationally, the demand for facilities for active recreation grew. The city responded by increasing the number of playgrounds and creating the Newton Recreation Department to organize and supervise programs. The needs of golfers meanwhile were served by no fewer than seven local clubs, all private and all dating from the mid-1890s.

In the 1890s, the full potential of the Charles River as a recreational resource for the public was recognized. As a result of two reports issued jointly with the Massachusetts State Board of Health in 1894 and 1896, the newly appointed Metropolitan Park Commission made its first taking on the banks of the Charles River: approximately 25 acres in Upper Falls that became the Hemlock Gorge Reservation. By 1900, the commission owned much of the land along the river in Newton, Weston, and Waltham, including the recreational facilities at Riverside that, with the privately owned park at Norumbega, attracted thousands of pleasure-seekers from all over Greater Boston.

The land for Islington Park in Auburndale was set aside as common open space in Alexander Wadsworth's subdivision plan for the North Auburn Dale Land Company in the 1840s. The photograph was taken in 1909.

Lincoln Park, shown here in 1909, was laid out as part of the subdivision at the foot of West Newton Hill in 1866. It was lost to the Massachusetts Turnpike in the early 1960s. The Second Church and old city hall are visible in the background.

For many years, the Newton Cemetery on Walnut Street served as a public park. In 1869, the year the three-arched, Gothic Revival gate was built, there were over 4,000 visitors. Designed by local architect George Meacham, the gate was demolished in the early 1950s.

Cold Spring Brook, which flows through the cemetery, made it possible to construct "the little chain of picturesque miniature lakes" that dominate the landscape. (Courtesy Newton Cemetery Corporation.)

Bullough's Pond is pictured here in the early 1880s, about the time that its inclusion in a "central park" was under consideration. Ice-cutting came to an end in 1886 when the pond was drained after a fire destroyed the gristmill at the outlet.

Bullough's Pond was restored for aesthetic reasons and recreational purposes in the late 1890s. The Newton Recreation Department "apparatus" is shown preparing the ice for skating in the 1920s.

"Cabot Woods," between Blake Street and the properties on the west side of Centre Street, would have been part of the proposed central park.

Part of Cabot Woods, Edmands Park was donated to the city by the heirs of J. Wiley Edmands in 1913. The pond, constructed as part of a WPA project in the early 1930s, is now in the last stages of eutrophication.

Farlow Park, Newton Corner, is seen here in 1888, shortly after the landscaping had been completed.

John Farlow bought William Kenrick's estate on Nonantum (now Farlow) Hill. He gave generously to the fund that established what became the Newton Free Library and then served on its board of trustees. He was one of five members of an 1876 Special Commission on Parks and later gave the land for Newton's first public park.

The public playground in Newton Centre was the city's first. Funds for acquiring the land and for the original plans by Frederick Law Olmsted were raised by the Newton Centre Improvement Association in the late 1880s.

This image shows a "Field Day" at the Newton Centre playground in the 1920s.

By 1913, when the Newton Playground Department was organized and the first commission appointed, most villages had a playground. In Newton Lower Falls, land leased for a playground in 1909 was bought with the help of a private donation in 1925.

In the early 1900s, the Newton Archers held "shoots" in the Newton Centre Playground.

"The boy without a playground is the father of the man without a job," stated Mayor Edwin O. Childs in 1915. These boys are playing football at Newton Centre.

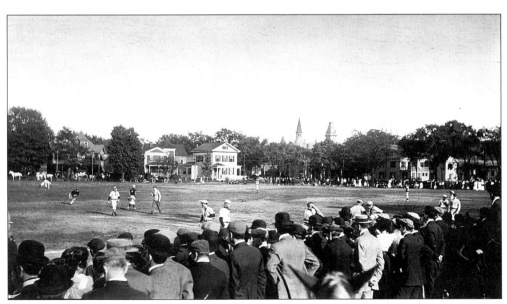

The West Newton Playground was a gift to the city from "some public-spirited inhabitants."

The playground in Cabot Park, shown here in 1910, was still used "not only by a large neighborhood population, but as an annex as well for sports for the boys and girls of the senior high school . . ." in 1925.

This "Field Day" took place in West Newton in 1920.

Crystal Lake can be seen in the 1880s, shortly after the completion of the Lake Avenue embankment that "reserved to the public a very accessible part of the shore."

"On the clearest and crispiest of winter days good ice brings out hundreds of skaters." *Historical Sketch of Crystal Lake*, 1911.

School playgrounds were used in and out of school hours. The former Peirce School in West Newton, built in 1895, was the first in Newton to be converted to apartments.

Vacation schools and Americanization classes at the Stearns School in Nonantum provided a "melting pot of the nations" for immigrants and their children. Built in 1907, it was demolished in 1977.

Additional recreational facilities for the young were provided by private institutions. Many of the students, boys and girls, black and white, attending Nathaniel T. Allen's West Newton English and Classical School, boarded at his home on Webster Street where this picture was taken.

The Walker Home for Missionaries' Children was started in 1868 when Eliza Walker, the widow of a foreign missionary, took in the children of friends while their parents were out of the country. The building on Grove Street burned in 1912, two years after this photograph was taken.

The popularity of golf soared in the 1890s. The Chestnut Hill Golf (later Country) Club was laid out in 1897. Bought by the city in 1982, it is now the Newton Commonwealth Golf Club. The Eliot Memorial in the foreground was dedicated in 1896 to mark the 250th anniversary of the Reverend John Eliot's mission.

One of three golf clubs in the city that no longer exists, the Newton Golf Club was located on the present site of the Boston College Newton campus on Centre Street from 1895 until 1916.

Miss Cobb and Mr. Kilburn relax on the Charles River in the 1890s. By that time, the river was no longer used as a source of power, and the recommendations of landscape architect Charles Eliot that it "be devoted to the use and enjoyment of the public as a drainage channel, an open space, a pathway, a chain of playgrounds, and a boating course" were finding acceptance.

Cora Cobb took this photograph of the "spot not far upriver from the Newton waterworks" where she and her friends used to picnic in the early 1900s.

The boys are fishing in the "upper Charles," *c.* 1891.

Half the funds for buying Auburndale Park were "contributed through the liberality of the citizens" of the village. It was one of the city's earliest acquisitions on the river.

In 1895, the year after issuing its first joint report with the Massachusetts State Board of Health on the improvement of the Charles River, the Metropolitan Park Commission acquired Hemlock Gorge in Upper Falls. Echo Bridge, in the background, had been completed 19 years earlier. (Courtesy Library of Congress.)

The Spaulding sisters of Newton Highlands and Edith Cobb of Newton Upper Falls were photographed in the Hemlock Gorge Reservation, c. 1902.

By 1900, Metropolitan Park Police patrolled the Charles River at Riverside. In 1901, there were 4 drownings, 19 rescues, and no arrests.

5. BOULEVARD, CHARLES RIVER RESERVATION, NEWTON, MASS.

The Metropolitan Park Commission constructed several "boulevards" or "parkways" through its reservations, particularly along the Charles and Neponset Rivers. Nonantum Road was completed in 1915; five years later, Charlesbank was built to connect it to Newton Corner. The Perkins School for the Blind in Watertown can be seen on the left.

Pictured here is the Weston Bridge over the Charles River in Auburndale in 1904. Well before the Riverside Recreation Area and Norumbega Park opened in 1897, the proximity of several private and commercial boathouses attracted "canoes, rowboats, shells, and sailboats, filled with ladies and gentlemen, adding, with the delightful music, greatly to the natural charms of the scenery."—*King's Handbook of Newton*, 1889.

The Weston Bridge is seen here from the river. "The four stone arches which span the river, two on the Newton side and two on the Weston side of the city line, are so low that it is with considerable difficulty, attended with danger, that the canoes pass up and down the river."—City Engineer, 1907. The bridge was rebuilt in 1916.

Canoeing on the Charles.

Estimates of the total number of canoes in the so-called "Lakes District" at the turn of the 20th century vary between 3,000 and 5,000 in a single day.

AUBURNDALE BOAT HOUSE,

Gray & Frost, Proprs.

Boats to Let.

West of Riverside Station, next to Newton Boat Club.
General agents for the "Gerrish" Canvas Canoes.

J. R. ROBERTSON,

MANUFACTURER OF

LIGHT WEIGHT CEDAR

—— AND ——

Canvas Boats and Canoes.

OARS, PADDLES, SAILS, ETC.

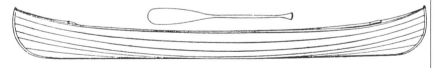

BOATS TO LET

At Riverside, on Charles River, rear Station,

And Terminus Commonwealth Ave., at Weston Bridge.

BOSTON & ALBANY R. R., 10 MILES OUT.

Address all correspondence to

Telephone Connection.   AUBURNDALE, MASS.

These advertisements from the Newton Directory in 1897 reflect the popularity of boating.

One of the earliest of several private boathouses belonged to the Newton Boat Club, organized in 1875. Besides a variety of pleasure boats, the members (200 in 1889) had the use of a bowling alley and a dancing hall.

By 1892, Lasell Female Seminary had a boathouse and "several boats upon the Charles River (which is within ten minutes easy walk) for the use of the pupils."

Perhaps the most widely publicized attraction in the area was the Commonwealth Avenue Street Railway's Norumbega Park. The photograph of the boathouses in the park was taken from what are now the grounds of the Boston Newton Marriott Hotel, looking upstream towards the bridge.

Besides the boating facilities, a restaurant, a theater, and eventually, the Totem Pole Ball Room, Norumbega Park had the largest zoo in New England.

NORUMBEGA PARK

AUBURNDALE
BOSTON'S POPULAR RESORT

Fliers such as this were issued by Norumbega Park to advertise its many attractions.

Five

SERVING THE CITY

In the years immediately after the Civil War, the population of Newton grew rapidly until, by 1870, it was one of the largest communities in Massachusetts that still had an open town meeting. Seven selectmen, elected annually, served also as overseers of the poor and surveyors of highways. Law and order were in the hands of constables, truant officers, and night police; fire equipment was manned by part-time crews who had to drop whatever they were doing to respond to an alarm; what would now be called an infrastructure was almost completely lacking. Though the town hall was in West Newton, the office of the town clerk, Marshall Rice, was still in his home in Newton Centre. Only the schools contributed to "the pride and joy" of Newton citizens. Early in 1873, the residents of Newton voted to adopt a city charter, and the last town meeting was held that November.

In his first inaugural address, Mayor James F.C. Hyde, warning of the ever-present possibility of taxable property being destroyed by fire, urged the newly elected aldermen and members of the common council to act quickly on the question of a municipal water supply. Discarding previous recommendations, it was decided to take water from the banks of the Charles River in Needham, pump it to a reservoir on Waban Hill, and distribute it from there. The first house connections were laid in 1877. The installation of sanitary sewers as part of the Metropolitan Sewer District began ten years later. Both systems, as well as tree planting, and the construction and maintenance of roads, parks, and playgrounds were the responsibility of the city engineer, whose office was created in 1874.

The willingness of private citizens to give time and money to provide services for their fellow residents was responsible for the initial organization of both the Newton Free Library and what is now the Newton-Wellesley Hospital. There had been several private libraries in Newton between 1798, when the West Newton Social Library began lending books to its members, and 1870, when, at no cost to the town, the library in Newton Corner opened its doors. Initially owned and administered by a board of managers and funded entirely by subscriptions and private donations, the library was transferred to the city in 1875. Similarly, in 1886, individual donors financed each of the small buildings that formed the nucleus of the Newton Cottage Hospital. Except for the Central Administration Building, all construction before 1927 was privately funded.

In 1849, when a final attempt to divide the town had failed, the town house in Newton Centre was abandoned; what had been the West Parish Meeting House on Washington Street became, after suitable alterations, the new town hall. Remodeled again, the building served as city hall until 1932 when, as Newton's first century of suburban development drew to a close, the new building in Newton Centre was dedicated.

In 1848, after town meetings had been held alternately in Newton Centre and West Newton for more than a decade, it was agreed to end the bitterness threatening to divide the town by moving the center of local government to West Newton. The West Parish Meeting House was bought and remodeled to serve as the town hall. In 1874, to the design of George Meacham, the old building was recycled once again to become Newton's first city hall.

James F.C. Hyde, a lineal descendant of Newton's fifth permanent settler, was the city's first mayor. In his inaugural address, he outlined a program for introducing new city services and, where necessary, updating those already in place.

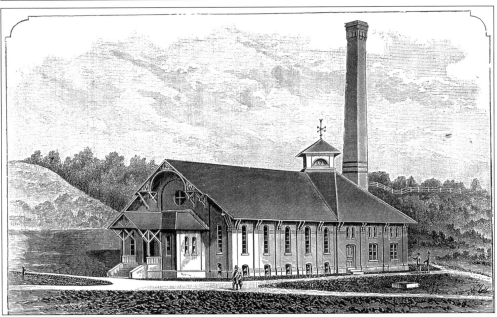

High on Mayor Hyde's list of priorities was a municipal water supply. By the end of 1877, water was being collected in filter basins along the Charles River in Needham, pumped to an open reservoir on Waban Hill, and distributed to homes in Newton Corner and Nonantum. The pumping station was on Needham Street, opposite the Oak Street intersection.

By the beginning of the 1890s, because the water supply was no longer adequate, the filter basins were extended and new conduits laid along the river to the pumping station in Newton Upper Falls.

The conduit near Kendrick Street in Needham was extended.

A second, this time covered, reservoir was built on Waban Hill. The surface of the masonry pillars and granite coping stones was covered with Portland Cement Plaster, "put on by Italian stone masons."

The distribution pipes connect with the reservoir in the circular stone gate chamber.

Fire Department Headquarters, Newton Centre, Mass.

This photograph of the fire department headquarters and center for the alarm system on Willow Street in Newton Centre was taken in 1896. It was largely due to pressure from the fire department that the need for a reliable water supply was regarded as a priority.

Hose No. 5 in Auburndale, like all other companies in Newton, was manned almost entirely by volunteers, in this case by two painters, a cobbler, a carpenter, and the village mailman. Reliance on "called firemen" lasted until the 1920s.

This fire apparatus was used in 1915 to fight the blaze that destroyed the Crystal Lake icehouse on Norwood Avenue. There had been commercial ice-cutting there for nearly a century.

The firehouse for Engine No. 1 and the Newton Corner police sub-station on Washington Street are seen in 1897. By 1900, three such sub-stations were located in firehouses.

In 1897, the police department and the local police court moved out of the city hall to the building two doors down on Washington Street, which had been recently vacated by the Peirce School.

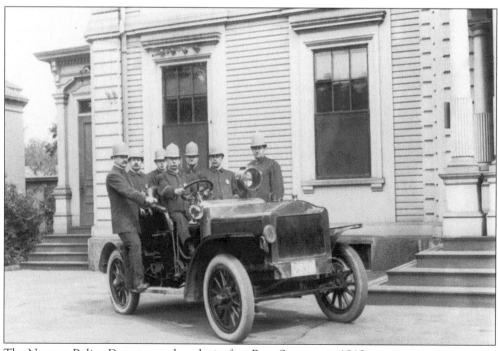

The Newton Police Department bought its first Ross Steamer in 1910.

The first police ambulance was bought in 1897.

The Founders Memorial Building, on the left, was designed by Kendall and Taylor for the Newton-Wellesley Hospital in 1908; the small buildings that constituted the original Cottage Hospital can be seen at the end of the drive.

The Claflin Guard, Newton's volunteer militia company, was organized in 1870 with headquarters in Nonantum House where this picture was taken. When the nearby Channing Unitarian Church moved across the tracks to Vernon Street in Newton Corner in 1881, the city bought the old building on Washington Street and converted it into an armory. As the C Company of the Fifth Regiment of the Massachusetts Volunteer Militia, the guards were called

upon to help during the Boston Fire in 1872 and were mustered into service in 1898, during the Spanish-American War. The men spent eight months in South Carolina, but did not leave the country. The company lost its identity during World War I and, in 1920, became part of the C Company of the 101st Regiment.

One of the many responsibilities of the city engineer was the construction and maintenance of hundreds of miles of roads. "The great increase of travel on some of our main streets has required a more durable surface than even gravel, and stone has been substituted to some extent, broken by a stone crusher."—Mayor J.F.C. Hyde, 1874.

"It has become a custom to water some portion of the streets . . . The practice possesses many advantages, aside from the comfort of our citizens, it is decidedly an economic measure for the preservation of our streets."—Mayor J. Wesley Kimball, 1885.

114

In 1909, no water was used on the streets, instead "dust layers in the form of emulsions were applied to macadam [crushed rock] or gravel roadways having a moderate traffic of horses or motor vehicles."—City Engineer.

"[T]he crushed rock road was standard and all right [*sic*] for steel tires and iron shoes. The auto with rubber tires tears it to pieces."—Mayor Edwin O. Childs, 1926. The solution was concrete or tarvia, shown here being applied to the surface of Commonwealth Avenue.

The Newton Engineering Department was responsible for the Newton half of the Elliot Street bridge over the Charles River in Newton Upper Falls. Thus, in 1897, when the streetcar company was granted a location across it, the city undertook to strengthen the piers and sagging arches, providing that Needham and the state paid their share.

Sewers, drains, and culverts were also attended to by the city engineer. The culvert shown under construction through the Newton Cemetery in 1929 was designed as a "permanent outlet" for some of the water of Cold Spring Swamp that eventually flowed into Bullough's Pond.

Young trees can be seen on Prince Street in West Newton at the beginning of the 20th century. "One of the reasons why Newton is so attractive and so often called the Garden City is the fact that it has such beautiful trees along most of its streets . . ."—Report of the Newton Forestry Department, 1910.

The Newton Forestry Department was organized in 1908. In 1909, there were 38,935 trees in Newton, nearly half on public land. They were sprayed when necessary for the elm leaf beetle, gypsy, brown tail and leopard moths, and the green-striped maple worm.

City workers in the "yard" on Crafts Street in 1909. The "new brick stables" were built in 1895 with wooden sheds for the teams and steam-rollers.

The first post office in Newton was opened in 1816 on Washington Street in Newton Lower Falls. In this 1883 photograph, the post office was located close by, in William Holden's store. Holden is standing in the doorway; the chapel offering free seats belonged to the Methodist Society. Remodeled in the 20th century, the building was razed during an urban renewal project in the 1970s.

The Newton Centre Post Office was located in Asa Trowbridge's store at the corner of Centre and Pleasant Streets for nearly half a century after it opened, *c.* 1827.

The Waban postman was photographed outside the local post office, then in E.W. Conant's store on Beacon Street. Street numbering "in anticipation of letter-carriers" began in 1888, and the first deliveries (in the Newton Corner district) were made later the same year.

By 1915, parcel post deliveries in Auburndale were motorized.

To comply with state law and to gather students, who had been attending classes in various locations, under one roof, Newton's first "pure high school" was built in 1859 on Walnut Street in Newtonville. Designed by J.D. Towle and renovated by George Meacham in 1875, it was replaced in 1896.

The editors of *The Newton High School Review* for 1885-86 can be seen in this photograph. The publication appeared monthly during the school year until 1922, when it was replaced by *The Newtonite*.

Newton High School on Walnut Street can be seen in this photograph, *c.* 1930. The "Classical High School" (Building One), built in 1896 to replace the original building, is on the right; the "Technical High School" (Building Three), built in 1909, is in the rear. Building Two was added in 1926. All were razed in 1972.

The Technical High School opened in 1909 "to increase and diversify educational opportunities."—Superintendent's Report, 1909.

The Rice School in Newton Centre was built in 1870 and named after Marshall Rice a few years before he died. The last of Newton's wood-frame schoolhouses, it was still in use in the 1950s.

The Class of 1889 poses outside the Mason School in Newton Centre. In 1959, the two schools were consolidated to become the Mason Rice School in a new building on Pleasant Street.

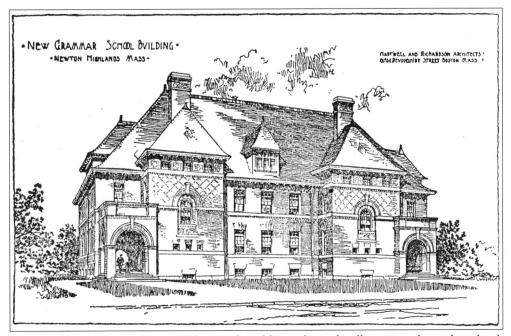

In the 1890s, the city began replacing the old wooden schoolhouses with modern brick buildings; many of them were designed by well-known Boston architects. The Hyde School in Newton Highlands, designed by Hartwell and Richardson, was dedicated in 1895.

Within a few years, an addition to the Hyde School became necessary because of the rapid growth of Newton Highlands. Third graders can be seen outside the new building in 1911.

Construction of the Main Library in Newton Corner was made possible in 1868 by the generosity of a group of public-spirited citizens. Financed initially by subscriptions and private donations, it was administered by a board of managers until 1875, when it was transferred to the city to become the Newton Free Library.

This photograph of the Reading Room in the Main Branch of the Newton Free Library was taken c. 1905. With several additions and alterations, architect Alexander Esty's Gothic Revival building served the Newton public for over a century. (Courtesy Library of Congress.)

In the 100 years after 1831, when Woodward and Ward completed their map of the town, Newton developed from a community of five small villages into a city with a population of over 50,000. In 1931, despite the misgivings of some who thought the project should "await more normal times," Mayor Sinclair Weeks decided to proceed with plans to replace the old city hall on Washington Street with a new building on Commonwealth Avenue that would include a War Memorial Auditorium. The architect was Charles Collens of Allen and Collens, the 10-acre site was landscaped by Olmsted Brothers, and the dedication, on November 11, 1932, was combined with the largest Armistice Day parade ever held in Newton.

ACKNOWLEDGMENTS

In writing *Newton, Massachusetts*, I have been able to draw on material assembled during research that preceded an exhibition *Newton the Garden City: The Growth of an American Suburb* held at The Jackson Homestead in 1988 to mark the Tercentenary of the incorporation of Newton as a town.

As with the exhibition, the book has been a cooperative effort of the Newton Historical Society and The Jackson Homestead: Margaret Latimer, the executive director, initiated the project and had the overall responsibility of seeing it through to completion; Susan Abele, curator of manuscripts and photographs, contributed technical expertise, an unerring eye, and knowledge of the collections that were indispensable.

All images are from the collections of The Jackson Homestead, except those acknowledged in the text. We would like to thank the organizations and individuals, particularly Joanne Baker, the family of the late Norton D. Clark, Russel Feldman, Steve Rosenthal, and the Newton Cemetery Association for permission to use their material. In addition, we wish to thank the City of Newton and its various departments for their help and cooperation over many years.

—T.F., 1999